Little
Pebble™

Holidays Around

# Kwan:

by Lisa J. Amstutz

CAPSTONE PRESS
a capstone imprint

Little Pebble is published by Capstone Press,
1710 Roe Crest Drive, North Mankato, Minnesota 56003
www.mycapstone.com

**Library of Congress Cataloging-in-Publication Data**
Library of Congress Cataloging-in-Publication data is available on the Library
of Congress website.
ISBN 978-1-5157-4855-7 (library binding)
ISBN 978-1-5157-4861-8 (paperback)
ISBN 978-1-5157-4879-3 (eBook PDF)
Summary: Explains how people prepare for and celebrate the holiday of Kwanzaa.

**Editorial Credits**
Jill Kalz, editor; Julie Peters, designer; Pam Mitsakos, media researcher;
Steve Walker, production specialist

**Photo Credits**
Capstone Press: Capstone Studio/Karon Dubke, cover; Dreamstime: Scott Griessel, 9;
Getty Images: Hill Street Studios, 5; Newscom: Hill Street Studios Blend Images, 15,
John VanBeekum/MCT, 7; Shutterstock: Candus Camera, 1, 22, 24, back cover, Enraged,
10, Pichugin Dmitry, 13, Svetlana Foote, 14, Timothy R. Nichols, 17, Uber Images,
11, xtock, 8 inset; The Image Works: E.A. Kennedy, 21, Thinkstock: Jupiterimages, 3,
Purestock, 19

Printed and bound in the USA.
000403

# Table of Contents

# What Is Kwanzaa?

Come together.

Light the candles.

Share stories.

Kwanzaa is here!

Kwanzaa is an African-American holiday. It is a time to give thanks.

Kwanzaa starts December 26.

It lasts seven days.

# Let's Get Ready

People make gifts.

They set out seven symbols.

Each symbol has a story.

The stories come from Africa.

A mat holds fruit and nuts.

Each child gets an ear of corn.

Everyone shares the unity cup.

The kinara holds seven candles.

One is black. Three are red.

Three are green.

# Kwanzaa Begins

Families light one candle each night. They talk. They share ways to help one another.

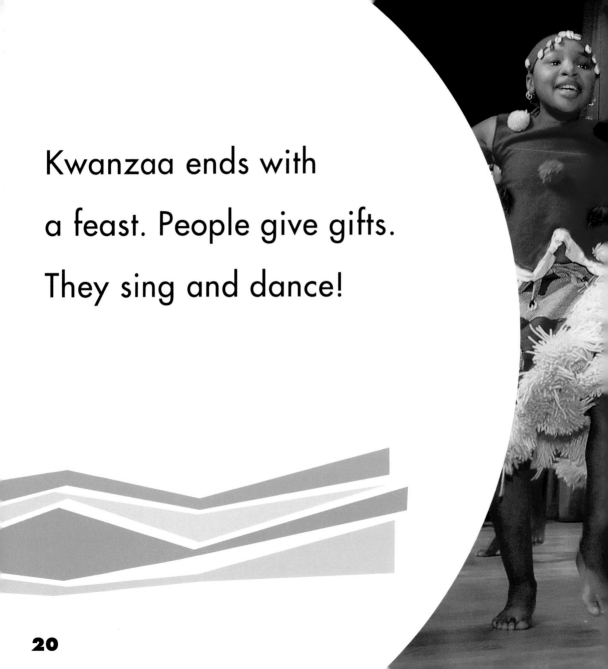

Kwanzaa ends with
a feast. People give gifts.
They sing and dance!

# Glossary

**feast**—a large, fancy meal for a lot of people on a special occasion

**kinara**—a candlestick used to hold seven candles at Kwanzaa

**symbol**—something that stands for something else

**unity**—being together as one